GEOTHERMAL ENERGY

Robyn Hardyman

CHERITON
CHILDREN'S BOOKS

Please visit our website, www.cheritonchildrensbooks.com to see more
of our high-quality books.

First Edition

Published in 2022 by **Cheriton Children's Books**
PO Box 7258, Bridgnorth WV16 9ET, UK

© 2022 Cheriton Children's Books

Author: Robyn Hardyman
Designer: Paul Myerscough
Editor: Victoria Garrard
Proofreader: Wendy Scavuzzo
Picture Researcher: Rachel Blount
Consultant: David Hawksett, BSc

Picture credits: Cover: Shutterstock/Pi-Lens; Inside: p1: Shutterstock/J. Helgason; p3:
Shutterstock/Zerzarbrab; p4: Shutterstock/Sergemi; p5: Shutterstock/Evgeniy Shvets;
p6: Shutterstock/Kris Wiktor; p7: Shutterstock/Steve Heap; p8: Shutterstock/Costazzurra;
p9: Shutterstock/U.J. Alexander; p10: Shutterstock/Andriy Blokhin; p11: Shutterstock/
SvedOliver; p12: Wikimedia Commons/Mark Johnson; p13: Shutterstock/ Sebastian
Studio; p14: Shutterstock/Zerzarbrab; p15: Shutterstock/Tanakornsar; p16: Wikimedia
Commons/Geothermal Anywhere; p17: Shutterstock/N.Minton; p18: Wikimedia Commons/
Ásgeir Eggertsson; p19: Wikimedia Commons/Rjglewis; p20; Shutterstock/Byelikova
Oksana; p21: Shutterstock/Yasemin Yurtman Candemir; p22: Shutterstock/Joseph Sohm;
p23: Photos courtesy of Pinewood Forest; p24: Shutterstock/Juan Carlos Martinez;
p25: Shutterstock/Anton_Ivanov; p26: Shutterstock/Alastair Munro; p27: Shutterstock/
KPG Payless2; p28: Shutterstock/ Johann Ragnarsson; p29: Shutterstock/Kavram; p30:
Shutterstock/Kange Studio; p31: Shutterstock/Fablok; p32: Shutterstock/Ronald Rampsch;
p33: Shutterstock/ Donatas1205; p34: Shutterstock/Cate_89; p35: AltaRock Energy, Inc;
p36: Eric Larson/Utah FORGE; p37: Shutterstock/Evgeni Fabisuk; p38: Shutterstock/Kiev.
Victor; p39: Shutterstock/SARIN KUNTHONG; p40: Shutterstock/Suleyman ALKAN; p41:
Shutterstock/Prehistorik; p42: Shutterstock/J. Helgason; p43: Shutterstock/Filip Fuxa; p44:
Shutterstock/Fabio Lamanna; p45: Shutterstock/Dotted Yeti.

Printed in the United States of America

Contents

CHAPTER 1

What Is Geothermal Energy?

Geothermal energy is heat within Earth. When we stand on the ground, we cannot feel it, but deep beneath our feet, there is heat—and a lot of it. This heat results from the way the planet is made. Fortunately for us, it is always there. The energy industry has realized that this heat is a precious resource, **which we can use to provide the power our planet needs.**

Cleaner Energy

Geothermal energy is part of the solution to our need for **cleaner energy**. At the moment, more than half of the energy the world uses comes from burning coal, oil, and natural gas in **power plants**. Coal, oil, and natural gas are called **fossil fuels**. We extract them from the ground, but they are in limited supply, so they are called **nonrenewable**. It took millions of years for them to form, so we cannot replace them.

This hot steam is rising from deep underground, where **groundwater** is heated by the surrounding rock.

Burning fossil fuels in power plants to make electricity creates harmful gases that are trapping Earth's heat and warming our **atmosphere**. This is causing changes to the **climate** around the world, and it can have catastrophic effects on life on Earth. Scientists tell us we must urgently reduce our use of energy sources that create harmful **emissions**. The heat in the ground is an energy source that produces no harmful emissions, because nothing is burned. We simply use that heat directly, or change it into electricity. We call this energy source geothermal power.

Layers of Earth

Earth is made up of four major layers. On the outside is the crust. This is the solid rock that we live on. It is 15 to 35 miles (24 to 56 km) thick under land. Under the oceans, it is thinner: about 3 to 5 miles (5 to 8 km) thick. Below the crust is the

mantle, which is a much thicker layer of solid and molten (melted) rock, or magma. This is about 1,800 miles (2,897 km) thick. Below that is the outer core, which is 1,500 miles (2,414 km) of incredibly hot magma. At the center of Earth is the core, about 1,500 miles (2,414 km) across and made of solid iron. The temperature at the core is about 10,800 degrees Fahrenheit (5,982 °C)—as hot as the sun's surface. The temperature of the rock decreases toward the outer layers, so that where the mantle meets the crust, it is about 392 degrees Fahrenheit (200 °C).

The crust is not solid. It is broken into pieces called tectonic plates. In places where they meet, the magma rises closer to the surface. The rocks and the underground water there absorb the heat from the magma. That is the heat that we can harness for geothermal energy.

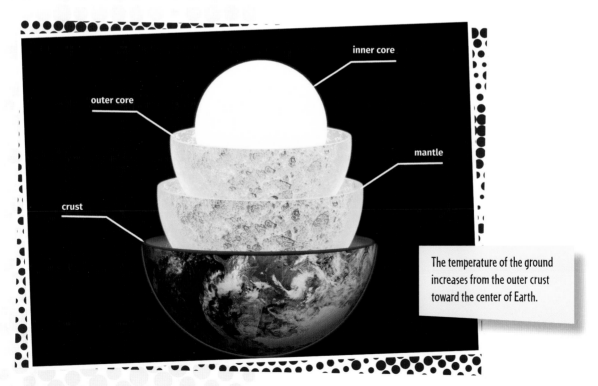

inner core

outer core

mantle

crust

The temperature of the ground increases from the outer crust toward the center of Earth.

How Does It Work?

Earth is constantly being warmed by its core, and the heat spreads upward through the layers of rock. That heat source is constant, so it is a renewable **source of energy. It will never run out. There are three main ways that we harness and use geothermal energy. All of them have a part to play in building our** sustainable **energy future.**

Using the Heat

The first method is to take heated water from below the ground and use its heat. The water rises to the surface at hot springs, or gushes up into the air in spurts called geysers. We can use the hot water directly, for example, in swimming pools, or we can use its warmth for other purposes, such as heating buildings.

The second method is to use the underground heat to warm or cool water. The water moves through pipes laid underground, then it moves up to the surface where its heat can be used for heating or cooling buildings.

At this hot spring in Yellowstone Park, heated water rises to the surface. The colorful areas around it are **bacteria** that live in the warm water.

The main disadvantage of geothermal energy as a source of electricity is its cost. It is very expensive to drill miles down into the ground, and often the exploratory drilling does not find a usable supply of heat. This has caused some energy companies to decide not to develop geothermal energy. Even when they do find a supply of heat that can produce enough steam, there is always the risk that the steam may run out at a particular site if the underground water supply is limited.

The third way of using geothermal energy is to use the underground heat and hot water to **generate** electricity in a power plant. That electricity is then fed into the **grid** and distributed, or sent out, to homes and businesses. This allows anyone to benefit from this clean and renewable energy source. They do not have to have their own geothermal **installation** to access it.

Good for the Environment

Geothermal energy has a low impact on the **environment**. The first two methods of using it have almost no negative effects, because they are not **intrusive** and nothing is burned. Some scientifically significant geothermal sites are very beautiful. The hot springs and geysers bubble up from the ground, so they are protected by law from ugly extraction equipment. Geothermal power plants are much less **polluting** than plants that burn fossil fuels. They emit, or give off, almost no harmful gases into the atmosphere.

This drilling rig is mobile and can be fitted to a truck.

CHAPTER 2

Heating and Cooling

We have seen the amazing temperatures that lie deep underground, but you do not have to dig very far to find ground that is warmer than on the surface. Just 10 feet (3 m) below us, the temperature of the ground is about 55 to 60 degrees Fahrenheit (13 to 15.6 $^{\circ}$C). That temperature remains constant all year round, whether it is winter or summer above ground, and we can use that heat for heating and cooling our buildings.

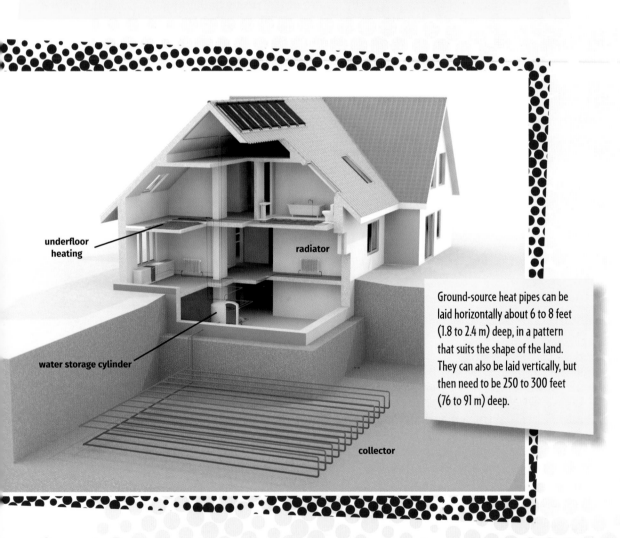

underfloor heating

radiator

water storage cylinder

collector

Ground-source heat pipes can be laid horizontally about 6 to 8 feet (1.8 to 2.4 m) deep, in a pattern that suits the shape of the land. They can also be laid vertically, but then need to be 250 to 300 feet (76 to 91 m) deep.

Ground-Source Heat Pumps

The way that we extract the heat underground for our own use is by using a ground-source heat pump. This is connected to a series of pipes buried underground. The pump pushes a fluid, often water, through the pipes. Down below, the water is heated by the ground. As it returns to the building, that hot water is then used to heat the building. This is done by passing it through a heat exchanger, which transfers the heat into the building's existing air handling and distribution system. If a **desuperheater** is added, it can be used to heat the building's water. The water then returns to the ground much cooler and is heated again.

Cooling It Down

This simple-but-effective technology can also be used to cool a building. If the air temperature is higher than the constant temperature below ground, the water in the pipes will be hotter above ground. It is pumped back into the ground, where it loses that heat and comes back up cooler, to cool the building. So, with geothermal, you have both heating and cooling for the cost of one system.

Sending Out the Heat

Geothermal heat can also be used another way, by drilling even deeper underground. Two **wells** are drilled, and water is pumped into one of them. It is heated by passing through rock underground, then pumped back up through the second well. Its energy is extracted and distributed to buildings to supply heat. This is called district heating.

This is the ground-source heat pump. New apartment buildings are being built with geothermal heating and cooling systems that serve all the apartments in the building.

BIG Issues
How Much Does It Cost?

The heat pump is not very expensive, but installing the pipes underground can be. A large and deep hole needs to be dug outside the building, which can be difficult in places where many people live. Once the pipes have been installed, though, and the hole filled in, the system should work for many years and not need to be disturbed. Over time, the system more than pays for itself by greatly reducing household bills.

Straight from the Ground

Another type of geothermal system uses groundwater heated by natural processes that take place below Earth's surface. This hot water can be pumped for a wide range of uses.

Underground Hot Water

The groundwater heated by the activity in the rock below ground can be as hot as 200 degrees Fahrenheit (93 °C) or more. The heat comes from areas where there is volcanic activity, or where tectonic plates meet and move slightly against each other.

In some places, such as at Yellowstone National Park, for example, the **reservoirs** of heated groundwater reach the surface. The result is a hot spring or a geyser. We can pump this hot water either from the surface or from a short depth underground, and use it in many different ways.

Glenwood Springs in Colorado is the world's largest hot-spring-heated swimming pool.

To tap into hot groundwater, a well is drilled. A pump can be added to bring the water to the surface, or it may rise up on its own. The hot water can be piped through a heat exchanger to remove its heat for use, or it can be used directly. Its many uses include swimming pool heating, space heating and cooling, heating tap water, and even heating roads and sidewalks to melt snow in winter.

Heating Whole Neighborhoods

Areas with hot water near the surface are fortunate to be able to use that water to heat buildings across a whole district. The water can be piped directly to nearby offices, schools, and homes.

The country of Iceland, for example, has a lot of underground hot water reservoirs, and many hot springs and geysers on the surface. In the capital city of Reykjavik, a district heating system uses this hot water to provide heat for most of the buildings across the city.

Once its heat has been used, the water may need to be returned underground to refill the reservoir by being pumped back below ground. In some cases, though, the reservoir will naturally refill itself from the water in the surrounding rock. In locations where there is heated groundwater not too far below the surface, it is an excellent way to produce geothermal energy at a relatively low cost.

Reykjavik, the capital city of Iceland, uses a lot of geothermal energy to heat buildings by using a district heating system.

Where Can It Go?

The beauty of using the heat in the ground or in groundwater directly to heat and cool buildings, is that it can be used just about anywhere. As long as there is space to drill into the ground to access its natural heat, geothermal energy can get to work.

All Types of Buildings

Ground-source heat pumps can be installed in all types of homes, whether single units or apartment buildings. One system can serve all the apartments in the building, with the advantage of spreading the installation cost among many consumers. The heat pump unit is about the same size as a traditional heating and cooling unit, and it is quiet to run, with no noisy fans. Ground-source heat pumps are ideal for public buildings such as schools. The pumps require very little maintenance and have no exposed dangerous equipment, such as open flames or fuel storage tanks. Since no fuel is burned, there are no harmful emissions given off.

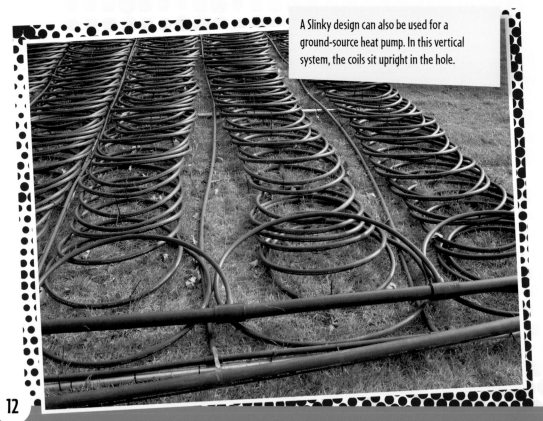

A Slinky design can also be used for a ground-source heat pump. In this vertical system, the coils sit upright in the hole.

The heat pumps continue working in all types of weather, from snow to sunshine.

Fast and Simple

Installing a ground-source heat pump system is not a complex operation. Depending on the condition of the soil and the amount of pipes required, a typical installation with horizontal pipes can be completed in two days. A vertical installation takes a little longer and costs more, because it drills down deeper, but it can still be done in a few days.

Horizontal or Vertical?

Installing a horizontal system is simpler than a vertical system, but it requires longer lengths of pipe to extract the heat needed for the system. The pipes are laid out in trenches, so more land is required than with a vertical system. If the ground is very hard, a vertical installation is more suitable as it requires less digging. Since the pipes go deeper, the ground is hotter, so less pipe is needed to extract the same amount of heat.

BIG Issues
Combining Old and New?

Most people have an existing heating system in their homes, often a **furnace** that burns gas. Replacing this entirely is a big commitment. Fortunately, ground-source heat pump systems can be added to these existing systems, so they can work alongside each other. The geothermal system will be the main heating system, but the furnace can kick in to supplement, or add to, the heating in extremely cold weather if needed.

Industry and Agriculture

There are many processes in industry that require either hot water or heat, or both. Geothermal energy can be the perfect way to deliver those in a clean and sustainable way. It is also widely used to help farmers grow and process their crops for our food supply.

Geothermal Energy in Industry

Industries use a massive amount of heat in their processes, so this is a huge area of opportunity for geothermal energy. It is particularly suitable for processes that need constant but relatively low heat, or for preheating liquids or materials before a high-heat process. The uses of geothermal energy in industry vary greatly, from drying timber and dyeing fabric to extracting gold and silver from rock. For example, **paper mills** use geothermal energy for all stages in their production process. The heat left over is used for drying wood. Drying is the most common industrial use of geothermal energy. This needs a relatively low heat to be applied over a long period. It is widely used for drying fruit and vegetable products to make them last longer.

Geothermal Energy in Agriculture

Geothermal water is also very useful in agriculture. Heating greenhouses with geothermal water helps maintain a constant temperature, resulting in a more reliable crop and faster-growing plants. The water in the pipes can also be released into the air inside the greenhouse, raising humidity,

This geothermally powered greenhouse in Iceland allows the farmer to grow crops that would otherwise not be possible during the long, cold winter.

The fish in this farm are contained in warm geothermal water.

or heat and water vapor, if necessary. The latest **innovations** allow systems to be adapted, or changed, to suit the types of plants being grown. So, a grower of roses can have a system with good air flow and low humidity, while someone growing plants that require a lot of humidity and heat can have a higher overall air temperature.

Geothermal water is also used to keep the soil in open fields at a steady, warm temperature. The farmer runs **irrigation** pipes under the soil, delivering water and heat to the crops. Geothermal water can also be used to kill pests in the soil that damage crops. This is usually done using steam, because a high temperature is needed to kill the pests. A plastic sheet over the soil keeps the heat inside.

Geothermal Energy in Aquaculture

Another use of geothermal energy is in aquaculture, or the farming of fish and other water animals. Warm water is used to spur the growth of animals such as alligators, shellfish, and tropical fish. Fish farmers around the world, from the United States to China and Japan, use geothermal energy in their work.

CHAPTER 3

Electricity from Heat

The third way geothermal energy contributes to our energy supply is by using the steam from deep underground to generate electricity. This happens in a geothermal power plant. The electricity can then be fed into the grid, and distributed to homes and businesses in the usual way.

Super Hot Work

Generating electricity from geothermal power needs water or steam at high temperatures of 300 to 700 degrees Fahrenheit (149 to 371 °C). The power plant must be positioned close to an underground reservoir of hot water or steam that is not more than 1 or 2 miles (1.6 or 3.2 km) down from the surface. A deep well is drilled down into the reservoir, and the hot water is piped up to the surface. There, it is used to power a **turbine** that generates electricity. In a different power plant design, two wells are drilled. Cool water is injected into the ground through one well, and the heated water is brought to the surface through the second one. Since the wells are so deep, the high pressure below ground keeps the water in a liquid state, even at such high temperatures. It becomes superheated steam as it rises toward the surface.

A Difficult Job

Geothermal steam requires no fuel, and the technology of the power plant is quite straightforward, so this keeps the costs down. The most expensive and challenging part of the operation is the drilling. Once an energy company has identified a location it thinks might be

Energy companies drill test wells like this one, to find the best places to develop geothermal energy.

suitable for a geothermal power plant, it must drill test wells to see if the conditions are right. There are not very many places where everything will come together in an ideal way. It requires an area with plenty of geothermal activity deep underground, usually where tectonic plates meet each other, and a natural reservoir of very hot water. Setting up a plant involves working with extreme temperatures and extreme pressure. Both of these are challenging, since the equipment needs to be made sturdy enough to **withstand** them.

Geothermal power plants must be located in areas where their impact on the environment will not be too extreme.

BIG Issues

What About the Environment?

Geothermal power plants do not burn fuel, so they do not emit harmful gases into the atmosphere. They also do not use up precious resources. The water and steam that they bring up from deep underground is pumped back into the ground after it has been used to generate electricity. The impact of these plants on the environment is, therefore, mostly visual. Their locations must be chosen sensitively, so they do not affect areas of natural beauty. They are best suited to areas that are not **densely populated**.

Dry Steam or Flash Steam?

In the world of geothermal energy, there are three main types power plants. All of them use the very hot water that is sitting in reservoirs up to 2 miles (3.2 km) below the surface, but in different ways.

Dry Steam

A dry steam power plant pipes the steam directly from the depths and up to the plant, where it turns the **generator** turbines, producing electricity. The basics of this technology are not new, although they have been improved over the years.

The first power plant of this type was built in central Italy more than 100 years ago, at a location where steam naturally spurted from the ground. There was no need to dig a very deep well. Since then, dry steam power plants have changed to bring up the steam through deeply drilled wells.

These plumes of water vapor are rising from the Krafla geothermal power plant in Iceland.

In a binary cycle power plant, the water and the working fluid are kept separate, so there are almost no emissions into the air.

Flash Steam

The geothermal industry has developed a second power plant design. This is called a flash steam plant. Flash steam plants take hot water under very high pressure from deep inside the well and change it to steam at the surface. This is called the flashing. Then, that steam is used to power the turbines. When the steam has cooled, it becomes water again and is injected back into the ground to be used again. Today, most geothermal power plants are flash steam plants.

Binary Cycle

There is a third design that uses the idea of the flash steam plant, but instead of using the geothermal hot water to make steam, it transfers the heat in it to another liquid. The heat causes that liquid to turn into gas, the way water turns to steam. The gas is then used to drive the generator turbine. This design is called a binary cycle power plant. This design's advantage is that it can use water that is cooler than the other two, at around 225 to 360 degrees Fahrenheit (107 to 182 °C). The second liquid has a lower boiling point than water, so the heating water does not need to be so hot.

Underground reservoirs with water of a lower temperature, less than around 360 degrees Fahrenheit (182 °C), are more common than reservoirs with water nearer 600 or 700 degrees Fahrenheit (316 or 371 °C). Using the binary cycle design makes them workable for generating electricity, so they are likely to be more widespread in future.

CHAPTER 4

Where in the World?

There are currently about 24 countries around the world using geothermal energy to generate electricity in power plants. The decisions about their locations are based on the geology of the country, because there has to be an underground reservoir of very hot water to feed the plant. For more direct use of geothermal energy, however, such as taking heat directly from the ground to heat water and buildings, there is no limit to where this can be done. The ground is at a constant heat around the world.

Geothermal Heat in Kenya

The main barrier to developing geothermal energy is the cost. The start-up costs, or first costs, for exploring the best sites and drilling the wells are high. Once the operations are going, however, the running costs are relatively low. There are no expensive fuels to purchase and no emissions to be dealt with.

The high start-up costs have stopped geothermal energy growth in poorer countries where electricity generation could be possible. In Kenya in Africa, however, they generate about 50 percent of all their electricity from geothermal energy, and the country is one of the top 10 producers in the world. This is possible because there is a 4,000-mile- (6,437 km) long

At the Olkaria power plant in Kenya, hundreds of wells have been drilled into the hot rocks more than 1 mile (1.6 km) deep.

fault line running through the country, with a string of volcanoes along it. These are the perfect conditions for geothermal electricity generation, and the industry has been supported in its development. Kenya also uses geothermal energy for some of its agriculture. One important crop that it exports, or sells to other countries, is flowers. These are grown in large greenhouses that are increasingly being heated by geothermal energy.

Geothermal Energy in Turkey

The country with the highest level of growth in geothermal energy over the past 10 years is Turkey. There, the government is supporting the development of geothermal in every way. New power plants are being built, and there are projects for using geothermal heat for heating greenhouses for agriculture, and for providing district heating to thousands of households in cities.

BIG Issues

Help from Governments

Since the costs of setting up a geothermal energy plant are so high, some governments have been supporting the geothermal industry with financial **incentives**. These can include reducing **taxes** for the plant operators or paying them a higher-than-standard price for the electricity they supply. The industry argues that it is important for these incentives to continue if geothermal energy is to grow as a large supplier of our energy needs.

This large greenhouse in Turkey grows vegetables and fruits using geothermal energy.

Energy in the United States

The United States is the world leader in producing geothermal electricity. It has the correct geology for geothermal power plants on the western side of the country, and it started using geothermal power many years ago. The country is also committed to developing the industry, not only for electricity generation, but also for direct uses.

The Mammoth-Pacific geothermal power plants are at Casa Diablo on the Sierra Nevada mountain range in California. These plants generate enough power for about 40,000 homes.

Western States Producing Power

In 2017, seven states had geothermal power plants: Hawaii, Nevada, Utah, California, Oregon, Idaho, and New Mexico. The biggest contribution by far, more than 70 percent, comes from California. The second-biggest producer is Nevada. The electricity these seven states produce is enough to power about 3.5 million homes.

There are only two known underground resources of steam in the United States: The Geysers in northern California and Yellowstone National Park in Wyoming, where there is a well-known geyser named Old Faithful. Since Yellowstone is protected from development, the only dry steam plant in the country is at The Geysers. There, the largest geothermal plant in the world has been built, with 22 geothermal power plants drawing steam from more than 350 wells. The country's other plants are either flash steam plants or binary cycle plants. On the Big Island of Hawaii, about 30 percent of its electricity is provided by a geothermal power plant at the Puna Geothermal Venture. The Hawaiian Islands are a volcanic hot spot, so conditions there are perfect.

Geothermal Heating

The United States has been slow to develop geothermal energy as a source for heating homes and businesses, but there are some new projects that are using this sustainable technology. Pinewood Forest in Atlanta, Georgia, for example, is an all-new community being built close to Pinewood Atlanta Studios, where movies are made. Each of the 1,300 homes will be heated and cooled by a ground-source heat pump system. This makes Pinewood Forest the first large-scale geothermal community in the country.

Even More Power

Many people in the United States are working hard to develop the country's geothermal energy industry. The United States Geological Survey (USGS) has estimated that there are still significant undiscovered resources in the western part of the country. These need to be investigated so that part of the renewable energy industry can grow. The experts think that geothermal power could eventually provide more than 10 percent of the country's total energy needs.

At the new Pinewood Forest residential development in Atlanta, Georgia, all the homes are heated and cooled by geothermal energy.

Energy in Latin America

According to experts, there are areas of Latin America with great potential for geothermal electricity generation. But so far, only about 5 percent of that potential is being used. The countries in this region really need an affordable and clean solution to their energy needs, and some of them are leading the way.

Costa Rica First

Costa Rica was one of the first countries in the region to develop geothermal energy. By 2015, about 13 percent of its energy generation was geothermal. There are fewer than 5 million people living in this small nation, but it is still one of the top 10 geothermal energy producers in the world.

Big in Mexico

Mexico also started developing geothermal power some years ago, and it is now the fourth-biggest producer in the world after the United States, Indonesia, and the Philippines. It aims to meet 35 percent of its energy needs with geothermal power by 2024. There are 25 volcanoes in the

At this crater in Costa Rica, hot gases rise to the surface from the heated water and rock below.

These geysers rise out of the ground in the Atacama Desert in Chile.

BIG Issues
A Reliable Supply

Countries in this region are developing other renewable energy technologies, such as **solar** and wind power. This is great, but using geothermal energy directly to heat and cool buildings has a big advantage over those technologies. Unlike sunshine and wind, the heat in the earth is constant. It can be relied on to be the same all the time. This means that a regular, reliable source of energy can be guaranteed, making geothermal energy much less risky.

country, which means there are plenty of underground reservoirs of hot water. The experts say that if these are properly managed, they could last for more than 100 years. The government has given a lot of public money to the development of science, technology, and innovation projects, and many are now in progress.

Other Central American countries, such as El Salvador, Nicaragua, and Guatemala, are also pushing forward with developing geothermal energy. At a conference on energy in Central America in 2018, experts highlighted the great opportunities it offers in the region, both for electricity generation and for direct use. It could bring great **economic** benefits by providing not only energy, but also jobs to people living in poor areas.

Slow in South America

In contrast to other areas of Latin America, the countries of South America have been slow to get started. Chile, for example, has the largest undeveloped geothermal area in the world in the Andes mountains. Chile's first geothermal power plant has recently opened, and everyone hopes it will encourage others to follow. In Argentina, some farmers are using geothermal heat directly to heat their greenhouses.

Energy in Asia

Many parts of Asia are on fault lines in Earth's crust, which makes them suitable locations for geothermal power plants. As a result, some of the biggest geothermal energy producers are in that region, and there are exciting innovations taking place there.

Power in the Philippines

The Philippines was one of the world's first big players in geothermal energy. The country's first power plant, at Mount Malinao, opened in 1979. It is still in operation today. By 2025, 12 new wells will be drilled at the plant to provide an extra 20 percent more steam. Another important geothermal plant is underway at Kalinga in the north of the country. Today, geothermal energy produces about 14 percent of all the country's electricity.

Indonesia

Indonesia has the largest potential for geothermal resources in the world. Scientists have identified 331 possible locations for power plants across the country. In 2018, it overtook the Philippines to become the second-biggest producer of geothermal electricity after the United States. The government is setting ambitious targets for the future, too, to knock the United States off the top spot. To achieve that, Indonesia needs more than 10,000 skilled workers in the industry, so it is working together with the Netherlands to share knowledge and set up a geothermal study and training program.

Mount Sinabung in North Sumatra, Indonesia, is one of the country's many volcanoes.

The Matsukawa Geothermal Power Plant in Japan is the country's first **commercial** geothermal power plant.

Energy in Japan and China

In Japan, a lot of people have been against large-scale geothermal projects because some of the best locations are in environmentally sensitive areas or tourist destinations. However, many smaller plants are in operation in some areas of Japan. As the use of nuclear power declines in Japan, the government wants to support new geothermal projects.

In China, in contrast, geothermal energy has taken off like a rocket. The country began its geothermal journey fewer than 10 years ago, but it already has the most geothermal district heating systems in the world, providing heating from deep geothermal wells. Most heating in Chinese buildings is provided by burning coal in furnaces, but this is very polluting. Therefore, the government is anxious to remove as many harmful emissions as possible to improve the country's air quality.

China is collaborating with, or working with, other countries to push its geothermal energy even further. Early in 2019, the Beijing Research Institute of Uranium Geology (BRIUG) signed a cooperation agreement with Arctic Green Energy, a company based in Iceland. They will work together to locate and develop geothermal electricity generation projects in China.

Energy in Europe

The spread of geothermal power across Europe is patchy. Not many areas have the geology suitable for electricity-generating power plants, but geothermal is more widely used for heating, especially in the colder countries. Like the rest of the world, the European Union (EU) is looking closely at the role geothermal energy can play in reducing the region's overall emissions, and providing Europe with clean energy.

In less than 50 years, Iceland has changed from being completely dependent on **imported** fossil fuels to having a renewable energy supply for almost all its heating and electricity.

Making Electricity

There are 117 geothermal power plants in Europe—16 of those only started operating in 2017, so it is a growing industry. Iceland is one of the biggest geothermal players in Europe. This small island nation sits on a tectonic boundary and is home to some very powerful volcanoes. This makes it possible for six power plants to operate in a relatively small area. The other countries where underground reservoirs of heated water are generating electricity are Germany, Italy, and Turkey. In fact, Turkey produces the most geothermal electricity of any country in Europe.

Geothermal Heating

In parts of central Italy, farmers have been using water heated by geothermal energy for hundreds of years to help grow their vegetables in the winter. Today, vegetable growers in Hungary get 80 percent of the energy they need from geothermal sources. Across Europe, greenhouses and fish farms use water heated by the ground for the heat they need to run their businesses.

The people of Europe need heating in their homes and businesses, too. District heating has an increasing role to play, and nine new heating plants started operating in 2017 in the Netherlands, Italy, and France. In Paris, for example, more than 1 million homes are supplied with geothermal heat by district heating. Individuals are turning to ground-source heat pumps for their heating, too, with almost 2 million units now installed. New housing developments are now much more likely to consider installing those as the main source of heating and cooling.

BIG Issues
Polluting Poland

Poland is the European country with the greatest dependence on coal-fired power plants for its electricity, and therefore, it is a major polluter. If the country could turn away from coal toward geothermal energy, it could make a huge difference to the level of harmful emissions coming out of Europe. Fortunately, there are some signs that this is starting to happen. The country has recently begun working with experts in Iceland and Norway to explore the potential for geothermal district heating in Polish homes and businesses.

In the Netherlands, cycling is a very popular form of transportation. Some places there have recently started using geothermal heat energy to keep bike lanes from freezing in the winter, so cyclists can ride safely.

CHAPTER 5

New Ideas

The geothermal energy industry is changing fast. New ideas are being developed in laboratories, offices, and on-site all the time. Around the world, experts are working together to share what they have learned, so this exciting technology can play an increasing part in our energy future.

Ground-Source Heat Pumps

Innovations are making geothermal heating systems more **efficient** and more attractive to potential buyers. At the 2017 European Geothermal Innovation Awards, the top award went to a company that makes a miniature **sensor** that explores the ground in detail before work begins.

It will help planners and designers develop advanced ground-source systems, and convince customers of the reliability of geothermal heating and cooling. The 2018 winner of the same award has produced an innovation that improves the efficiency of the heat pump in the deeper wells that are used for district heating.

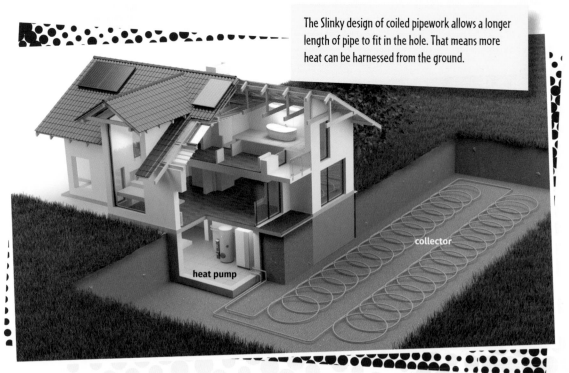

The Slinky design of coiled pipework allows a longer length of pipe to fit in the hole. That means more heat can be harnessed from the ground.

collector

heat pump

A Smaller Footprint

In residential geothermal systems, ground-source heat pumps are connected to a network of pipes underground. As water passes through the pipes, it is warmed by the heat in the earth. Creating an effective system requires a lot of pipework, and this has previously taken up a lot of space. However, one design innovation is helping to reduce the area needed. It uses pipework in a Slinky shape—flattened, overlapping coiled loops of pipe. This design fits more pipe into a smaller area. It means that these systems can be installed in more densely built places, such as inner cities.

The mineral magnesium can be extracted from the hot water that comes up from underground, then used for other purposes.

Harmful Minerals

In geothermal power plants, the very hot water that comes up from deep below ground through the wells contains high levels of **minerals**. These can slow system performance, by leaving **deposits** inside the heat exchanger that extracts the heat from the liquid. These minerals, such as magnesium, lithium, and other metals, build up over time, causing considerable damage. They are also very useful for other purposes, however, so it is a good idea to extract them.

The challenge is that the minerals in the liquid are at fairly low concentrations. After heat has been taken by the power station, the water is not above the ground for very long before it is pumped back down. Industry innovators are working on ways to extract the minerals without affecting the performance of the power station.

Better Drilling

The ground is hard! To access the heat beneath our feet, geothermal energy engineers need to drill deep down into hard rock, and that is a real challenge. Fortunately, there are companies with years of experience in drilling in oil fields, that are using their skills and knowledge to develop new drilling technologies for the geothermal industry.

Tough Equipment

The longer it takes to drill down through hard rock, the more expensive a well will be. More people and equipment have to be available for a longer period of time. Drilling through hard rock also wears out the end of the drill and the **motor** driving it, both of which are expensive. One oil-drilling company has successfully used an innovative drilling system to cope with these conditions. It uses a drill made of the strongest metal and an extremely powerful motor that can power the drill for many long hours to reach way down underground. The high temperatures there affect the equipment, but this system uses a very high-temperature **lubricant** in the drilling fluid to keep the drill working smoothly.

Conditions can be tough at the drilling site, and the equipment must be able to withstand them.

A laser is a highly concentrated beam of light. One recent idea in geothermal drilling is to use it to help break up the rock when drilling.

Using Lasers

Another innovation in drilling for geothermal energy uses a very different technology. A group of German and Swiss researchers have been testing a method called LaserJet drilling. This uses a laser, which is a very powerful beam of concentrated light, to help the drill get through very hard rock. The laser hits the rock before the drill, and it is contained within a jet of water. The laser energy starts to break up the surface, and the water blasts rock pieces out of the way so they do not damage the laser equipment. A traditional drill is then used to finish the job and to remove all the loose rock.

BIG Issues
A Lot of Benefits

The successful use of a drilling system that can cope with high temperatures, high pressure, and hard rock could have a huge impact. It means that many more geothermal resources that were previously unreachable can now be developed. It will also help businesses drilling for oil and gas, as well as the nuclear energy industry. The economic benefit of all this could be huge, creating jobs and bringing geothermal electricity to millions more homes.

Smart New Energy

Standard geothermal power plants need underground reservoirs of very hot water 1 to 2 miles (1.6 to 3.2 km) below the surface. That water is heated by the surrounding rock, which is very hot because it is close to the magma that rises from places where the plates of Earth's crust meet. Those places are fault lines. The problem with trying to expand the use of geothermal energy is that these natural underground reservoirs do not occur in many places.

Reaching That Heat

In the United States, for example, underground reservoirs are much more common in western states than elsewhere. Studies have shown, however, that there is enough potential energy in the hot rocks of the western United States to supply a large part of the country's total energy needs. One very important innovation in the geothermal energy industry is making it more possible for that to happen. That is the Enhanced Geothermal System, or EGS.

This geothermal plant is situated in Tuscany, Italy. Tuscany has underground reservoirs of hot water and was the site of the first geothermal power plant.

Amazing New System

The EGS involves pumping water into naturally occurring cracks in the ground 2 to 3 miles (3.2 to 5 km) below the surface. The water opens up the cracks slightly, so that new, human-made reservoirs are created underground. There, the natural heat of Earth heats the water to around 600 degrees Fahrenheit (316 °C). The hot water and the steam that is also created are then pumped back to the surface to a power plant. There, the steam is used to turn turbines that produce electricity. The hot water is cooled and sent underground to start the process over again. This closed system, which recycles the water, also ensures that water is not wasted.

The beauty of the EGS is that it can be used almost anywhere there is rock of the right type. One company in the United States has led the way in the development of EGS technology. It is called AltaRock, and it was founded in 2017 by Susan Petty. She raised more than $50 million in funding for research and development for her work. AltaRock is carrying out surveys in many areas across the United States. The company is looking for suitable locations for creating entirely new geothermal power plants in areas that were not previously possible. It is also looking at existing geothermal power plants, because EGS can also be used to make existing water reservoirs bigger and therefore more productive. This could completely change the geothermal energy industry and make it as important as solar and wind power.

The team from AltaRock is coming up with new ways to harness geothermal energy.

Cutting-Edge Research

The urgent need to reduce the levels of harmful emissions that are being created by our use of fossil fuels is driving governments, scientists, and industries around the world to support research into renewable energy technologies. Geothermal energy is part of that widespread effort, and there are many exciting developments taking place in laboratories and out in the field.

Pushing Ahead

The United States Department of Energy (DOE) has pledged millions of dollars to support cutting-edge research. In 2018, it chose a project at the University of Utah to receive up to $220 million over five years for research and development. The project is called the Frontier Observatory of Research in Geothermal Energy (FORGE). It is looking at ways to develop EGSs at a site outside Milford, Utah. Scientists and researchers are learning how best to engineer these human-made systems, by developing and testing new techniques, and collecting a massive amount of information. That type of creative technological innovation is not only necessary to advance EGSs, but it will also help to secure the country's energy supply. It will strengthen the United States' position as a world leader in geothermal energy.

This testing drill rig is part of Utah FORGE's work to investigate and develop the potential of EGSs.

Sharing Energy in Europe

In Europe, a major new research project was launched in 2019. This collaborative project has 19 partners across the EU sharing €17 million ($19 million) of funding. The aim is to develop technologies to allow geothermal power plants to respond to the changing demands for power from the electricity grid. This means looking at ways to store the heat energy when demand is low, so it can be released later when demand is high. Another part of the project is looking at ways to reduce the build-up of mineral deposits in the machinery at the power plant. These can affect the efficiency of the process, so solving that problem could even double the output from a power plant.

The DGE-Rollout project in northwestern Europe will bring geothermal heating to millions more people in Belgium, France, the Netherlands, and Germany over the next 10 years.

BIG Issues
Heating Homes

Renewable electricity generation is important. However, one of the biggest sources of harmful pollution in colder regions is the use of gas-fired furnaces to heat homes and buildings. Using deep geothermal energy for district heating has the potential to change that radically and is an urgent priority for the industry. A group of 10 companies in Germany, Belgium, and the Netherlands has started work on an EU-funded research project to develop deep geothermal energy (DGE) for heating in the region. A total of €18.7 million ($21 million) has been given to the project, which should result in new heating networks being built.

CHAPTER 6

Geothermal Energy Today

The growth in renewable energy over the past 10 years has been led by solar power and wind power. Geothermal energy has been growing, too, but at a slower rate. The high start-up costs of exploration and drilling have put some people off, but the benefits of geothermal power are becoming clearer all the time.

Energy All the Time

Once geothermal energy—either a power plant or a heating system—has been set up, the running costs are low. Over time, for example, heating your home using a ground-source heat pump will save a lot of money on utility bills.

On a bigger scale, one of the benefits of geothermal energy is that it is a reliable and constant source. Because the temperature underground does not change, that heat is always there to provide heating or to power an electricity plant. This is in contrast to solar and wind power systems, which produce less energy when the sun does not shine or the wind does not blow.

In 2019, the district of Meaux near Paris, France, won an award for its geothermal heating network, which extends over 20 miles (32 km) and serves 18,000 housing equivalents, including apartments, pools, hospitals, and businesses.

Success Stories

Although there is much more work to do, geothermal energy is already a success story. The experts say that the installed geothermal energy systems around the world are already making a huge difference in our environment. They are removing millions of tons of the harmful **carbon dioxide** produced by burning fossil fuels, making our air cleaner and helping in the fight against **climate change**.

The technology of geothermal energy is improving all the time. Governments and businesses are realizing its huge potential. They are setting up research-and-development projects to make it more efficient and cheaper. Businesses are seeing the advantage in buying their electricity from geothermal power plants, too. In 2018, for example, Coca-Cola announced that its bottling plants in the Philippines would be powered by geothermally generated electricity.

Big businesses such as Coca-Cola are beginning to invest in geothermal energy for their factories.

Hope for the Future

In 2018, the World Bank released a report on the status of geothermal energy in Latin America and the Caribbean region. The report found that geothermal energy could have a very important role to play in the region because it has huge **reserves** that are still mostly untapped. It pinpointed the problems connected with developing this technology and proposed real, workable solutions to them. A similar report by the United Nations (UN) on geothermal activity in Africa paints a positive picture of progress. These encouraging reports are likely to inspire others around the world to look to the heat beneath their feet.

A World Working Together

The story of geothermal energy has been one of pockets of development around the world. Some countries, such as Iceland, have been leading the way and learning the lessons needed for this technology to play a bigger part in the world's energy supply. Other countries are only just beginning to see the great possibilities that it offers. The good thing is that the countries with the knowledge are now beginning to share it.

Germany and Turkey

The last few years have seen some important agreements signed between countries. The German Geothermal Association (BVG) has, for example, signed a cooperation agreement with the Turkish Geothermal Power Plant Investors Association (JESDER). They want to work closely together to develop the technology and find business opportunities to use it. Turkey has the fastest-growing geothermal industry in the world at the moment, and Germany has a lot of technical skill. The two will work together not only on power generation, but also on the direct use of geothermal energy for heating and cooling in homes, businesses, agriculture, and industry. They will publish joint reports and hold conferences to share their findings.

This geothermal operation in Turkey is one of many new plants in that country, where geothermal energy is growing fast.

The United States and New Zealand

Another welcome agreement was signed in 2018 between the DOE and New Zealand's Ministry of Business, Innovation and Employment (MBIE). New Zealand has large geothermal resources and a long history of using them. Geothermal energy now provides about 17 percent of the country's electricity, but there is much more to use. New Zealand is aiming to have 100 percent of its energy from renewable sources by 2050. Although geothermal energy still makes quite a small contribution in the United States, the country has scientists with the expert knowledge needed to push it.

Joining Forces

The International Partnership for Geothermal Technology (IPGT) brings together experts from Australia, Iceland, New Zealand, Switzerland, and the United States. It provides a place where government and industry leaders can meet to learn from each other and work together on projects. This prevents the same mistakes from being made over and over around the world, so that geothermal energy can move forward as fast as possible.

BIG Issues
Keeping Control

As with any industry that has an impact on the environment, there needs to be a system of regulation, or checks and rules, for companies. This covers how permission is given for exploratory drilling, limiting the impact of drilling on a local environment, and rules about the quality control and maintenance of power plants. It is much easier to create rules that will work internationally if all countries come together to help shape them.

China and Belgium are also looking at cooperating on geothermal energy, using the research carried out by one Belgian research organization to help with site development in China.

Volcano Power

In the small country of Iceland, there is an exciting development in the technology of geothermal energy that could unlock a major new source of power. The country is already a world leader in its use of geothermal energy, not only for electricity, but also for heating homes and businesses. This time, they are looking at a geothermal system that goes deeper and hotter than ever before.

Using Volcanic Heat

Volcanoes usually occur in places where the tectonic plates of Earth's crust meet. Along these faults, the magma from deep underground rises closer to the surface. This magma heats the water in the underground reservoirs used in standard geothermal power plants. Now, though, three Icelandic energy companies have formed the Deep Drilling Project to go directly to the heat source and drill even closer to the magma itself. This is an enhanced geothermal project. There is no reservoir of water, but injected water heats to a very high temperature. The people working on the project want to find out if it is economically possible to extract energy from a system at this depth and temperature.

The volcanoes in Iceland erupt regularly, but geothermal engineers want to drill down close to the magma underground to create superheated steam.

Super Steam

The advantage of drilling so deep and to such a high temperature is that it creates "superheated steam." This is 400 to 600 degrees Fahrenheit (204 to 315.5 °C), and is dry steam—the ultimate find for geothermal energy. Dry steam contains 10 times more energy than standard wet steam. They would mean the same amount of power could be extracted from a smaller area, with less impact on the environment. It would also use fewer resources, so it would be cheaper.

Work at Two Wells

The first well was drilled at the Krafla volcano site and reached 1.3 miles (2.1 km) deep. Water was pumped down into it, and superheated steam arrived at the surface. This was the most powerful geothermal well ever drilled. But, sadly, it had to be shut down when a valve failed while attempting to connect the steam output to a generator.

A second well was then attempted. After 176 days of drilling, the well was 2.9 miles (4.7 km) deep. The temperature down there was a staggering 932 degrees Fahrenheit (500 °C). The well was lined with a concrete pipe, and water was pumped through it. Work continues at the well, with additional testing of this amazing new technology.

The knowledge gained by Iceland's Deep Drilling Project will be enormously useful to others around the world looking to develop high-temperature geothermal energy. Groundbreaking projects like that show the world the enormous capacity that geothermal energy has to power our world.

Iceland's Deep Drilling Project drilled its first well almost 3 miles (5 km) down into the Krafla volcano.

Evolutions of the Future

Today, less than 1 percent of the world's energy consumption comes from geothermal energy. Yet, we are literally standing on the solution to the problem of creating a secure and sustainable energy future for our world. Just a few miles down, the ground is hot enough to provide for all our energy needs. This energy source is constant, unlimited, and clean. We need to get going!

We Can Do It!

Why have we been slow to develop geothermal energy? It's because of a series of technical and engineering challenges, which we already have the ability to overcome. The challenges are in dealing with very high temperatures and high pressures, at deep distances underground. We have seen that the innovations of the last few years have been taking on these challenges.

We are finding new ways to reach the natural reservoirs of very hot water that are formed by volcanic and tectonic activity. We have also discovered how to create new reservoirs, by injecting water at high pressure into rock at great depths. This will allow us to build many more geothermal power plants to create our electricity. New homes, too, will increasingly be built with geothermal heating and cooling.

These geothermal hot springs are in Bolivia. Latin America has enormous potential for developing geothermal energy in the future.

Geothermal energy could one day be the power source that makes it possible for people to live on Mars.

Sharing Knowledge

As we build more geothermal power plants, the cost of them will fall. We are sharing the knowledge we have gained with partners around the world, so countries new to the technology will not make the same mistakes made by the first countries to use geothermal energy. Governments can provide financial help with the start-up costs and some security to deal with the risk of new projects not working out as well as hoped.

One perfect example of this way forward is the Mexican Center for Innovation in Geothermal Energy. A network of 150 experts from universities, private companies, and governments are working together at seven research institutions on more than 30 projects to create geothermal opportunities in Mexico and Latin America.

BIG Issues
Beyond Earth?

We have a long way to go to make the most of the geothermal energy that is sitting right here on Earth. But already, the International Geothermal Association (IGA) is thinking way, way ahead. At a conference in April 2019, they discussed the geothermal possibilities beyond our planet, out in space. Is there heat below the surface of Mars? What about on Jupiter's moon Europa, or Saturn's moon Enceladus? Maybe one day we will be able to go there and find the answers to these questions!

Glossary

atmosphere the blanket of gases around Earth

bacteria microscopic organisms

carbon dioxide a gas in the atmosphere that contributes to global warming

cleaner energy energy that does not pollute the environment

climate the regular weather conditions of an area

climate change the changes in climate around the world caused by the gradual increase in Earth's temperature

commercial related to making money

densely populated a place where a lot of people live

deposits substances put down in an area

desuperheater a machine in a geothermal heating system that allows the heat to be used for heating the water that comes out of the faucet

economic related to the money systems of countries

efficient able to achieve maximum productivity with minimum wasted effort or expense

emissions something, usually harmful, that is put into the air

environment the natural world

fault line a break in the rocks of Earth's crust

fossil fuels energy sources in the ground, such as coal, oil, and gas, that are limited in quantity

furnace an enclosed structure in which materials are heated to high temperatures

generate to make

generator a machine that converts energy into electricity

geology related to the structures on and beneath Earth's surface

grid the network that distributes electricity from power plants to consumers

groundwater water that is found below the ground, not at the surface

imported bought and brought in from another country

incentives things that encourage people to do something

innovations smart new ways of doing something

installation something that is put in place

intrusive annoying or unwelcome; causes problems

irrigation a system for watering crops

lubricant a liquid that helps two materials slide easily over each other

minerals solid, non-living natural substances that are found in the ground

motor part of a machine that provides it with power

nonrenewable will eventually run out

paper mills sites at which paper is made

polluting damaging the environment by releasing harmful substances

power plants places where energy is created

renewable describes energy created from sources that do not run out, such as light from the sun, wind, water, and the heat within Earth

reserves supplies still unused

reservoirs large pools of collected groundwater

resource something, such a geothermal power, that is available for use by people

sensor a device that detects something

solar from the sun

sustainable able to protect the environment by not using nonrenewable natural resources

taxes money paid by people and organizations to their country's government

turbine a machine used to convert the movement of air or a liquid into electricity

wells long shafts that reach into the ground to extract a resource

withstand remain undamaged or unaffected by something

Find Out More

Books

Bard, Mariel. *Geothermal Energy: Harnessing the Power of Earth's Heat* (Powered Up! A STEM Approach to Energy Sources). PowerKids Press, 2018.

Brearley, Laurie. *Geothermal Energy: The Energy Inside Our Planet* (True Books: Alternative Energy). Children's Press, 2018.

Lachner, Elizabeth. *Geothermal Energy* (Exploring Energy Technology). Britannica Educational Publishing, 2019.

Websites

Read all about geothermal energy at:
www.alliantenergykids.com/RenewableEnergy/GeothermalEnergy

Learn more about geothermal energy at:
www.ducksters.com/science/environment/geothermal_energy.php

Find out more about geothermal energy from the Energy Information Administration (EIA) at:
www.eia.gov/energyexplained/index.php?page=geothermal_home

Log on for the latest news and information on geothermal energy at:
www.thinkgeoenergy.com/about

Publisher's note to educators and parents:
All the websites featured above have been carefully reviewed to ensure that they are suitable for students. However, many websites change often, and we cannot guarantee that a site's future contents will continue to meet our high standards of educational value. Please be advised that students should be closely monitored whenever they access the Internet.

Index

About the Author

Robyn Hardyman has written hundreds of children's information books on just about every subject, including science, history, geography, and math. In writing this book she has learned even more about science and discovered that innovation is the key to our future.